LIVINGROOMS

VITAE PUBLISHING, INC.
GRAND RAPIDS, MICHIGAN

9130014

First published in the United States of America by:
Vitae Publishing, Inc.
50 Monroe NW
Grand Rapids, MI 49503
Telephone: (616) 459-7600
Fax: (616) 459-9075

Other Distribution by:
Rockport Publishers, Inc.
146 Granite Street
Rockport, Massachusetts 01966-1299
Telephone: (508) 546-9590
Fax: (508) 546-7141

ISBN 1-56496-239-3

Front cover image: M.L. Slovack Design, Inc.
Photographer: Hal Lott
Back cover images: (clockwise from top left) • Credit on page 68
• Janet Schirn Design Group, Inc.
Photographer: James Yochum
•Credit on page 57

Production by Sara Day Graphic Design

10 9 8 7 6 5 4 3 2

Manufactured in Hong Kong by Regent Publishing Services Limited

Living It Up: Designers on Living Room Design

Could there be a better era for living rooms? Top designers will tell you that the only taboos today are *the rules*. In the global village, styles and historical periods are blended with ease. Formality can be taken or left as needed.

Is this to say that anything goes? If so, what's a living room *for* anymore? In recent memory, living rooms were for formal entertaining, period. These days, individual lifestyles could dictate decor with the qualities of a medieval great room, a keeping room, a period room, a parlor, even a drawing room (keeping in mind that drawing rooms were rooms for ladies to withdraw *to*). Or all of the above. With endless possibilities for the living room now, how do contemporary designers arrive at solutions?

"Living rooms are my favorite thing to do," says designer Richard Himmel, "there is a greater latitude in 'living' than in the regimen of dining and sleeping." For Himmel, "checklist" and "standard procedure" are dirty words. The process of designing a living room, for him, is a collaboration with the client; "We normally design a living room for comfort and convenience, depending on the client's needs." Those needs are usually fleshed out by means of interviews with the clients.

Designer Janet Schirn asks a lot of pointed questions about how her clients aspire to live and how they *don't* want to live. "I observe what actually takes place in the home—how the kids interact when the phone rings, what the husband does when he comes into the house. If you make a living room responsive to what people do everyday, they will use it. Sometimes it only means that you need to put an ottoman with a chair."

Once Schirn has come up with as many functional furniture plans as she can, she asks the client, "When you come in with the newspaper on Sunday morning, where are you going to sit in this plan? Who will have your coffee with you? Will you do something different when it is summer or winter? By this time, we often have altered the way the client sees him or herself. Sometimes they're so surprised they want to change the way they live."

Designer Steve Tomar may even put a television in the living room, to insure that the client will use the room. "You try to put people into the room," he says, "a living room costs too much to go unused." Over the years, Tomar has gotten better at reading between the lines in client interviews; "They think that when their house is done, nothing is going to get dirty, or show wear, and that the children are all going to behave. But new decor doesn't change your life."

Ron Frey takes a lot of pride in *not* being a signature designer. "We don't want someone to be able to tell that the Frey company has been there. It's when people say to our clients, 'It's so YOU!' that we are successful."

Frey sees his mission as helping clients save money by protecting them from design mistakes. Putting the designer's ego last, Frey gives the client hands-on experience in selecting fabrics and such. "We don't do color boards. Instead, we have samples floating around, so that the client can lay them against one another. It is really messy, but it works better for us." In fact, Frey keeps his contract for accessorizing separate, believing that clients shouldn't do too much too soon. He likes them to live awhile in the newly designed room, and to see it at different times of day and in different lighting. The waiting period does the designer a world of good too, says Frey.

So, back to our question about what a living room is *for* these days? If the designer is as good a listener as he or she is a designer, there are simply no limits to what can happen. But one thing is certain: clearly, living rooms are for *living*.

— Alison Aves

Joanne Hutchinson Associates, Inc.

JOANNE HUTCHINSON, ASID
861 CANYON TRAIL
AKRON, OH 44303
(216)867-1311
FAX (216)867-1311

Wes Hageman
Interior Design

WES A. HAGEMAN, ASID
SIX MICHAELANGELO
ALISO VIEJO, CA 92656
(714)588-8213
FAX (714)588-8133

My clients and I design custom homes and interiors reflecting a common commitment to quality, detail, comfort, and lifestyle. With extensive experience in custom homes, I prefer to be involved in every phase of architectural planning, construction, interior design and decoration. Whatever the style, from a post-modern home in Irvine Cove, to an Italinate villa in Fairbanks Ranch, I bring professionalism and imagination to the project.

Photos: Eric Figge Photography

Carol Conway Design Associates

CAROL CONWAY, ASID
8242 E. DEL CADENA
SCOTTSDALE, AZ 85258
(602)948-1959

As a designer, I enjoy the special relationship I establish with my clients. I enjoy clients who take an active interest in their projects and who are open to new ideas. Ultimately, the designer must provide a client with service that guarantees availability and a project completed in a timely and professional manner.

Sharon Campbell
Interior Design

SHARON CAMPBELL, ASID
217 CRESCENT ROAD
SAN ANSELMO, CA 94960
(415)453-2323
FAX (415)461-3813

My clients tell me I listen: I hear the description they are giving of the concept they have in mind. I also observe their lifestyle, and this allows the concept to be translated into reality. When I begin to understand my clients, it becomes possible to put their spirit into their environment.

All Photos: David Livingston

Erika Brunson
Design Associates

ERIKA BRUNSON
903 WESTBOURNE DRIVE
LOS ANGELES, CA 90069
TEL. (310)652-1970
FAX (310)652-2381

Bartoli

DOUGLAS R. BARTOLI
825 SANTA BARBARA STREET
SANTA BARBARA, CA 93101
(805)963-6125
FAX (805)963-6127

Since the early 1970s, I have found great pleasure in working closely with clients in creating comfortable environments.

Houses with charming and engaging interiors do not just happen, they take years of diligent and loving involvement. They should look as if they have always been.

The places that we spend time in should be highly personal; filled with comforting colors, textures, forms and objects that help to recall those times and places that are brimming with sunny memories and simple pleasures.

When I work on commercial projects, I utilize these same values to give a sense of place in history, for in today's world, much of our time is spent outside our homes and these environments should also be comfortable, charming and welcoming.

Photos: James Chen

Arkules + Associates

BARBARA ARKULES
5224 EAST ARROYO ROAD
PARADISE VALLEY, AZ 85253
(602)840-7332
FAX (602)840-6459

LINDA ARKULES COHN
340 NORTH DEERE PARK WEST
HIGHLAND PARK, IL 60035
(708)433-5414

Below: "God Is In The Details." Design relates to desert landscape and Taliesin architecture. Custom seating of cactus green linen (partially shown) follows curve of linen-covered wall. Base, of same mahogany used throughout, floats, subconsciously widening narrow room. Seating also provides sleeping area. Integrated table/chest at end holds bed linens. Cushions, pillow heights and channel quilting of leather repeat block's 8" height. Custom, curved lighting and furniture restate circular architecture.

Opposite: Henry Moore sculpture sits on custom terrazzo table. Modular table adapts to other sculpture. Terrazzo flooring flows to custom banquettes' bases and integrated corner table that wrap around two walls. Terrazzo's flecks are repeated in bespoke rug. Like black base of Arp sculpture, black silk upholstery acts as visual base for larger works of art. Seating can be reconfigured to focus on concert grand piano (not shown) or to accommodate various social functions.

Thomas C. Achille & Associates

THOMAS C. ACHILLE
521 NORTH LA CIENEGA BLVD,
SUITE 10
LOS ANGELES, CA 90048
(310)659-0300
FAX (310)659-7981

A timeless blend of classic and contemporary elements, related to the client's own personal style is the hallmark of Thomas C. Achille & Associates.

Below: Diverse elements, including a David Hockney painting, French limestone fireplace and antique needlepoint carpet create an international ambiance for a Beverly Hills living room.

Opposite, above: Space, light and classic architectural elements frame a serene blend of contemporary and period pieces for a grand living room in Los Angeles' Windsor Square neighborhood.

Opposite below: Painstakingly restored, this venerable Paul Williams estate in Hancock Park includes elaborately detailed draperies and upholstered furnishings to enhance an exceptional collection of signed antiques.

Photos, above: John Vaughan; opposite: Mary E. Nichols

Standish Design, Ltd.

DEBBIE CLINE STANDISH, ASID

We are dedicated to creating comfortable, distinctive and enduring interiors, reflective of our clients' lifestyles and objectives.

LaBarge, Inc. –
Metternich Cole

DALE METTERNICH
1353 BRIDGE STREET NW
GRAND RAPIDS, MI 49504
(616)392-1473
FAX (616)392-5001

Interior design should reflect the personality or philosophy of the individual or organization which will utilize the space. A designer should be a catalyst, making personal dreams a reality.

Upper right: "Room With A View." Sun room of summer cottage in Saugatuck, Michigan. Bavarian styled log cabin overlooking the Kalamazoo River, the connecting link between Lake Michigan and inland yacht basin. Mirrored wall reflects the panoramic view with comfortable sofas and eating area for leisure times.

Right and opposite: "Brookby Estate." Unusual L-shaped grand scaled living room designed for comfortable entertaining, quiet areas for afternoon teas, completely adaptable for club meetings and chamber music concerts. Color keyed to accentuate the 1930's gilded paneling and polished parquet floors, both a "must keep".

Winnie Levin Interiors, Ltd.

WINNIE LEVIN
595 ELM PLACE, SUITE 202
HIGHLAND PARK, IL 60035
(708)433-7585
FAX (708)433-9353

I am dedicated to creating comfortable, distinctive and enduring interiors reflective of the client's lifestyle.

It is very important to provide my clients with a balance between interior architecture and carefully selected furnishings, while always giving the utmost importance to detail.

The most successful projects always evolve through a close working relationship with my clients, where I can anticipate their needs and wishes and translate them into the kind of home they dream of.

Inez Saunders and Associates, Inc.

INEZ SAUNDERS
449 NORTH WELLS STREET
CHICAGO, IL 60610
(312)329-9557
FAX (312)329-9093

Our goal is to meet and succeed in reaching the individual needs and tastes of each of our clients. To obtain this goal, we keep in close communication with our clientele and run a very professional and efficient office.

Top: A contemporary high-rise provides a dramatic backdrop for elegant living.

Bottom: The addition of a sunroom provides a visual connection to the outdoors and gives an open feeling to this home.

Above: Renovated Old World
living-dining room now exists in
what was once a high school
classroom.

Jayne Dranias
Designs

Jayne Dranias, ASID
1438 North Monroe
River Forest, IL 60305
(708)771-9352
FAX (312)222-9091

I strive for timelessness in design, working closely with clients and guiding them to achieve the best design for their lifestyle. Such as, introducing contemporary art and accessories into a traditional setting.

After many years in the field of interior design, it has convinced me that quality and comfort are the most important features for timelessness!

Above top: Overlooking the vast vista of Lake Michigan, the unusual details of the oval sitting room with its quasi-Byzantine arches form a striking background for the contemporary furnishings and abstract art. The earthen tones of the monochromatic color scheme and minimal use of the varying textures create a strong unifying mood for this unusual setting.

Above: This library combines regency, directoire and contemporary furniture for view of hearth over which hangs an antique portrait. The color scheme is keyed to the antique Persian area rug. Using cranberry striae wallcovering on the ceiling and book niches solidifies the light oak paneling. Please note that the herringbone parquet was placed on the diagonal as the area rug and furniture - highlighting the corner fireplace.

Opposite: Elegant fabrics and richly toned walls complement the architecture of this magnificent room. English and French furniture combined with contemporary pieces create an aura of European grandeur. Fine antiques and art are reminiscent of the "grand tour."

Jackie Davis
Interiors, Inc.

JACKIE DAVIS
3755 EAST 82ND STREET, SUITE 100
INDIANAPOLIS, IN 46240
(317)577-1116
FAX (317)578-1907

Jackie Davis Interiors, Inc. takes pride in having no "signature" style, but is known for its use of color and the solving of unique space planning problems.

Our designers seek to achieve the highest level of aesthetics and functionality, while working within each client's guidelines and project limitations.

We share the belief that attention to detail, a striving for creative excellence and special follow-up service are the keys to each successful interior.

Above opposite: A hand-painted trunk and memorabilia from many travels fill this den.

Below opposite: This living room's furnishings were placed to facilitate entertaining, conversation and recitals.

Above: Dramatic architecture and accents of rose, yellow, periwinkle and black enrich the living/dining areas of this lakeside home.

Lawrence Boeder
Interior Design

LAWRENCE BOEDER
445 EAST WISCONSIN
LAKE FOREST, IL 60045
(312)613-6640

Most of my work involves traditional, understated design. My staff and the range of talented craftsmen I employ as resources, appreciate the need for quality and beauty. The result we are seeking is comfortable and never dated. Happily, each project is as distinctive as each client's own personality and lifestyle.

Above top: Traditional residential setting.

Above: For homes in Lake Forest, Illinois.

Opposite: Special setting where antiques, collectibles and pieces come together in a Lake Bluff, Illinois home.

Busch and Associates

F. MARIE BUSCH, ASID
1615 NORTH MOHAWK
CHICAGO, IL 60614
(312)649-9106
FAX (312)649-9106

My approach to interior design is to be individualistic, understanding, flexible and creative in meeting client needs. Much thought goes into the coloration of each assignment, as well as fabric selection, and where possible, architectural detailing, to establish comfortable and timeless grace for every client without repetition of design ideas.

Opposite below: "Cochise" the howling coyote sets the tone for this whimsy filled porch, a favorite summertime retreat.

Opposite above: Capitalizing on an already dark room, the deep green walls create a serene setting for a smallish living room and present the perfect backdrop for "Hairdresser" a 1948 painting by Russian-born Simka Simkhovitch.

Above: A large, sunny living room, made intimate by the use of dark green walls and dramatic shapes.

Stedila Design, Inc.

JOHN STEDILA
TIM BUTTON
175 WEST 93RD STREET
NEW YORK, NY 10025
(212)865-6611 FAX (212)865-
5021

PHILOSOPHY:
A sense of timeless style, a fastidious attention to detail, and a commitment to creating highly personalized spaces in which to live or work—these are the hallmarks of Stedila Design, Inc.

Right and below: A golden master suite, spare yet elegant, serves as an inviting private retreat in this Palm Beach, Florida, home.

Left: An opulent salon ideal for entertaining in the grand tradition.

Below: A renovated barn has been transformed into a casual retreat for a New York family.

Charlotte Moss & Co.

CHARLOTTE MOSS
1027 LEXINGTON AVENUE
NEW YORK, NY 10021
(212)772-6244
FAX (212)734-7250

PHILOSOPHY:
By emphasizing the basic elements
of comfort and by balancing scale,
color and detail, we create interiors that reflect the lifestyles of our
clients. A strong collaborative
relationship with our clients cul-
minates in surroundings that are
elegant, distinctive, personal and
functional.

Juan Montoya

JUAN MONTOYA DESIGN
CORPORATION
80 EIGHTH AVENUE
NEW YORK, NY 10011
(212)242-3622
FAX (212)242-3743

Right: Designer Juan Montoya evoked the spirit of the 1920s in his own New York apartment. His extensive art deco collection is exemplified in the French inlaid cabinet and silver vase in the background. The 19th century Italian stone vase and the 18th century Italian Rococo table are among the many eclectic objects displayed against this backdrop.

Below: An extensive remodeling project produced large public rooms that flow into one another to allow for flexible entertaining. The art deco-inspired furniture in the dining and living areas was designed by Juan Montoya.

Above opposite: In this New York residence, a newly married couple gave the designer complete creative freedom, bringing only their art collection from their previous homes.

Below opposite: Evocative of the art deco luxury liners of the 1920s and '30s, this New York apartment extends its nautical feeling through expansive views to the East River.

Juan Montoya

Left: A dining area is created through the addition of a platform in the existing living area. A color palette of stone and turquoise is used to accent architectural details and lighten dark spaces.

Below: Through the careful manipulation of space and lighting, designer Juan Montoya achieves a sensitive balance between the functional needs of his client and the appropriate display of his client's extensive art collection.

Opposite: Fabric wall hangings bring continuity to this two-story space, allowing for an intimate backdrop for the furniture around the fireplace. The fireplace, center table, chairs, pedestals and carpet were all designed by Juan Montoya.

David H. Mitchell
& Associates

DAVID H. MITCHELL
1734 CONNECTICUT AVENUE NW
WASHINGTON, D.C. 20009
(202)797-0780

PHILOSOPHY:
Our work is often perceived as modern, but we would rather not be pigeonholed into one style of design. We like to mix things up, using old with new, contemporary with antique and costly with inexpensive.

Our clients have a strong sense of style. As designers, our responsibility is to interpret and develop their ideas into a workable plan that reflects their personality.

Healing Barsanti Inc.

PATRICIA HEALING
DANIEL BARSANTI
243 EAST 60TH STREET
NEW YORK, NY 10022
(212)753-0222

DANIEL BARSANTI

Gandy/Peace, Inc.

CHARLES D. GANDY, FASID, IBD
3195 PACES FERRY PLACE NW
ATLANTA, GA 30305
(404)237-8681
FAX (404)237-6150

WILLIAM B. PEACE

Below: Texture is the key word in this comfortable, but subtle, informal living space. Diverse fabrics complement the sisal flooring and underscore the richness of the antique Chinese bamboo underwear, which is mounted on a custom cherry rod with bronze finials.

PHILOSOPHY:
Capturing each individual client's spirit through simplicity, drama and classicism, we emphasize comfort and function in creating interiors that become canvasses for people, artwork and accessories through professional adeptness in lighting, detailing and creativity.

Above left: An antique Biedermeier secretary sits in contrast to an overscaled contemporary painting in this quiet and elegant living room. A pair of French chairs, upholstered in a delicate needlepoint, offer versatility by floating between two sitting groups.

Left: A subtle mix of damask against damask contrasts with the simplicity and strength of the deKooning drawings in this comfortable setting.

Sandra J. Bissell Interiors

SANDRA J. BISSELL, ASID
93 MAIN STREET
NORTH ANDOVER, MA 01810
(508)475-2060

Right: The serenity of the French blue and cream color scheme enriches the antique furnishings, among them a large gateleg oak table from the early 19th century.

PHILOSOPHY:

A room that looks as if it had evolved over time, gracefully accepting new acquisitions and beloved old possessions, furnishings that enhance rather than fight the architecture—this is the best of design.

My focus is on collaborating with my clients, interpreting their desires, incorporating their needs, and creating interiors that reflect their unique personal style.

Underscoring the esthetics of any interior design, must be an understanding of what makes a room comfortable and livable. Sensible space planning; proper use of scale, color, texture and pattern; attention to detail; and a generous infusion of creative ability elevates a room from the ordinary to the elegant, from trendy to timeless.

Above: Effective lighting and custom-designed upholstery in rich tones of caramel, wheat, terra cotta and ebony complement the patina of the aged oak paneled library walls.

Left: Fine paintings by Boston masters enhance the fireside seating area. The antique Georgian mahogany game table is graced by four classically inspired chairs faux painted to suggest satinwood, walnut burl and ebony.

Van Hattum & Simmons, Inc.

PETER VAN HATTUM
225 EAST 60TH STREET
NEW YORK, NY 10022
(212)593-5744

HAROLD SIMMONS

The three most important "givens" for any job are the space itself, the client's personal style, and last but not least: a realistic budget. The architecture of a space very much influences the choice of decoration and furnishing, as do the budget considerations. But the most successful rooms happen when mutual understanding and trust develop between client and designer. Although styles change with time, fads are for fashion, whereas decorating is a major investment and should endure.

Opposite: A Manhattan living room with deep red glazed walls, English Regency furniture and antique Bessarabian Rug over sisal floor-covering. The painting is a Seventeenth Century landscape attributed to Claude Loraine, in original frame.

Below: For a country house in East Hampton, linens and cottons were used with a striped braided wool rug, a mixture of French and English country antiques and a collection of antique Delft. The room is square with a high "tray" ceiling and white glazed rough wood walls.

Ellen Sosnow
Interiors

ELLEN SOSNOW
850 PARK AVENUE
NEW YORK, NY 10021
(212)744-0214

I love doing residential interiors, especially ones that look old, comfortable and just a little bit seedy. I especially like uphol-stered furniture you can sink into. I enjoy clients who take an active interest in their projects and who are open to new ideas.

Sanders/Kalow
Designs Limited

RENEE SANDERS KLEIN
880 FIFTH AVENUE
NEW YORK, NY 10021
(212)7447405

NANCY KALOW
301 EAST 75TH STREET
NEW YORK, NY 10021
(212)249-1149

As designers, we enjoy the special relationships we establish with our clients. Our first priority is to analyze the space and make it fulfill the client's needs. We pride ourselves on designing rooms that are not only functional, but beautiful as well. We strive for elegance and comfort and always use these elements in a fresh, artistic and enduring way.

Above: The lacquered tortoise shell walls against the custom oak cabinetry (that was designed to showcase this rare Pre-Columbian art collection) gives this study a warm glow.

Opposite above: A sweeping view of city lights surrounds this duplex penthouse designed for nighttime glamour.

Opposite below: Soft tones and textures enhance the comfort of gracious living.

Charlotte Moss & Co.

CHARLOTTE MOSS
1027 LEXINGTON AVENUE
NEW YORK, NY 10021
(212)772-6244

Designing is a partnership for me. The challenge is to work with a client to create a result that reflects their personality, supports their lifestyle and maximizes the unique character and potential of the house or apartment in the most creative, comfortable and distinctive way. Achieving a "personal style" for each client is the hallmark of our group, projecting their individual flair and cachet rather than a result that is easily identified as the designer's work.

It is crucially important to know and understand the client well if we are to anticipate their needs and wishes and translate them into the kind of home they dream of . . . comfortable, beautiful, inspiring, personal, and practical!

Brian McCarthy/ Parish–Hadley Associates, Inc.

BRIAN MCCARTHY
PARISH–HADLEY ASSOCIATES, INC.
305 EAST 63RD STREET
NEW YORK, NY 10021
(212)888-7979

A successful concept should begin with the development of an interesting and appropriate architectural background. I like to share in this phase of the client's planning, rather than beginning at the furnishing stage.

Decoration should be a record of the client's lifetime of looking, collecting and refiningùan evolution of inborn taste together with the expansion of interests and intellect. I try to express the persona of the client and to create the ômagicö that goes beyond just a competent job.

image dennis krukowski

Healing Barsanti Inc.

PATRICIA HEALING
DANIEL BARSANTI
243 EAST 60TH STREET
NEW YORK, NY 10022
(212)753-0222

Our interiors have to work for the client. By interpreting their needs and wants, a finished space will reflect their personality and lifestyle. It is our job to use quality materials and attend to the details which make for pleasant and lasting interiors.

B. Jordan Young Inc.

BETTYE JORDAN YOUNG
8570 HILLSIDE AVENUE
LOS ANGELES, CA 90069
(213)650-0101

A great space is a theater for life. It is important that the production be built around a team effort. Egos must take a back seat in order that function and value be established as efficiently as possible. As the bones of the set, the architecture has to be responded to and respected. Proportion and detail, color and light go hand-in-hand in streamlining and enhancing the theme. Knowing what is not needed is oftentimes as important as what is. Communication is everything in producing a comfortable, almost second skin fit. Good design, like a favorite piece of music, is never tiring.

Clare Fraser
Interior Design

CLARE FRASER
127 EAST 59TH STREET
NEW YORK, NY 10022
(212)737-3479

Butler's of Far Hills, Inc.

JEFFREY B. HAINES
BOX 516
53 ROUTE 202
FAR HILLS, NJ 07931
(908)234-1764

Rooms should appear as if they evolved as opposed to decorated overnight. I enjoy giving a room this feeling of evolution and personality. It is very important that the client's wishes are achieved, but most important, that the client looks and feels at home in their home. I enjoy color and the use of it in large amounts and the subtleties of stretching the color palette in a room. I feel that dissonance in color and texture and formality in a room are vital to achieve a room that appears as if it has been a natural evolution of purchases and acquisitions throughout the years.

Tomar Lampert Associates

STEPHEN TOMAR, ASID
STUART LAMPERT
8900 MELROSE AVENUE, SUITE
202
LOS ANGELES, CA 90069
(310)271-4299
FAX (310)271-1569

Good designers, in addition to being creative, should also be editors and coordinators. As designers, we try to understand our clients' ideas, dreams and needs in order to express them in good aesthetics and a functional environment.

Our approach is to treat interiors the same way an actor treats each role; individually rather than playing the same part each time.

We work in contemporary and traditional styles, incorporating authentic and honest elements. Good design should not become dated, and as time passes we strive for our interiors to become more classic. We like to update past works to maintain a freshness and continuity.

We take pride in our detailing and planning of interior architectural elements such as lighting, built-in cabinets, space planning, finishes and backgrounds. Many of our assignments are designed in conjunction with the client's architects and builders.

Below: Living room with tropical color tones.

Opposite, above: Country modern family room.

Opposite, below: Family room provides easy living.

Photo: Kim Sargent 1991

Photo: Philip Thompson

Photo: Chuck White

Hilary Thatz, Inc.

CHERYL DRIVER
38 STANFORD SHOPPING CENTER
PALO ALTO, CA 94304
(415)323-4200
FAX (415)323-8300

I specialize in the grandly classical as well as the cozier style of European country. My rooms are romantic and comfortable and never take themselves too seriously. I look for good bones in a room and if they don't exist, I delight in creating architectural detail. An antique or two is essential for adding character and heritage to a room that might otherwise look too new. I like uncontrived contrivance—a clutter, a certain disarray, to make the room look instantly lived in.

Above: Trompe l'Oeil pediment adds whimsy to this reclusive musician's study.

Below: A view of a sunny country house corner.

Opposite: Voluptuous window treatment beckons a young musician to the work at hand.

Photos, above: David Livingston, opposite: John Vaughan

Sanchez-Ruschmeyer Associates, Inc.

CARLOS SANCHEZ
AL RUSCHMEYER
151 VERMONT STREET, #11A
SAN FRANCISCO, CA 94103
(415)252-6080

The design process is fascinating. The formation of a partnership to exchange ideas and explore clients' needs brings out aspects of their personalities that enable us to create homes reflecting personal style.

This collaboration results in homes that are warm, rich, inviting and most of all, comfortable.

Our work is as varied as our client list. Our personal style? Environments that reflect a mood and atmosphere of ease an graciousness.

Partners for over twelve years, our work is guided by appropriateness to architecture and suitability to the client's lifestyle.

Our reward is the pleasure we take in seeing delight in our clients' faces as they enter a completed room for the first time.

Photos, above: John Vaughan; below and opposite: Eric Zepeda

Billy W. Francis
Design/Decoration, Inc.

BILLY W. FRANCIS
964 THIRD AVENUE, 11TH FLOOR
NEW YORK, NY 10155
(212)980-4151
FAX (212)980-4842

Right: Hand-stenciled walls in shades of beige help this large (40' x 30') living room appear warm and comfortable.

Below: A rare combination of freshness and sophistication is achieved in this comfortable Ridgewood, New Jersey, living room.

Akins and Aylesworth, Ltd.

MARILYN AKINS, ASID
DONNA AYLESWORTH, ISID

Our approach to design considers the client's personality and lifestyle, as well as the architecture, in determining the style direction of the project. We like to enhance the client's taste preferences and raise them to a level beyond which even the most sophisticated client may have imagined.

We love clear color, sometimes using it boldly, sometimes softly, always considering what colors are most flattering to the client.

We aim for warmth and comfort, preferring to accessorize with antiques. Although creativity is our forté we pride ourselves in being good business people as well.

Young & Company

JAMES BOYD YOUNG

Above: French and English influence for a seasonal house in Florida.

Below: Part of a collection of historical equestrian paintings assembled in the main house of a Kentucky horse farm.

Opposite: Side niches created to give scale and balance to a Florida living room. Linen and silk against the colors of a pool.

Index of Interior Designers